MW00973485

ELIZABETH SOWELL

Ingredients Of Singleness

First published by IngramSpark 2021

First edition

ISBN: 978-0-578-84688-0

This book was professionally typeset on Reedsy.
Find out more at reedsy.com

To all the singles that need a reminder that they're amazing and deserve to live as spiritually free and unapologetic as possible.

Acknowledgement

I have to acknowledge God first; if it weren't for His guidance and the path He directed me on, none of this would have occurred. I want to thank my mother, father, and grandmother for rearing me in the Word, redirecting me when necessary, and being the living example of what it means to be a follower of Christ. I want to give a specific shout-out to my mother, who gave me the push I needed to jump into this project and trust God to lead me. I want to thank Dee, Sam, and the Adventure Squad for keeping me grounded and reminding me that life is something to be enjoyed. I want to thank my Aunt Shonte and Reverend Napier, who encouraged me that my singleness is not in vain and to use this time to be the best servant I can be. I want to thank Reverend Carla Satterthwaite for helping me accept my calling and providing me with the opportunity to do what God called me to do. I want to thank my spiritual siblings, Mahdi and Candace, for encouraging me not to be afraid of what the Lord has for me and reminding me of who I am in Christ. I want to thank the Spiritual Mavericks and Chloe and Taneesha for keeping me in prayer, being shoulders to cry on, encouraging me to dig deeper into studying the Word, and being a robust spiritual support system. I want to thank The Content Chicks for all the work they've done to help me establish this. I want to give a special shout-out to my colleagues, who reminded me of the importance of self-care and generally being awesome people. Finally, I want to thank the rest of my family, friends, church family, and loved ones for putting up with my shenanigans and standing by me.

Thank you, and I love you all!

I

Spiritual Development

Introduction

One of the most important things you should know is that everything has a function. Merriam-Webster's dictionary defines "function," the noun, as a purpose natural to or intended for a person or thing, and the verb, to work or operate in a proper or particular way. So, how does that relate to singleness? Simply put, your singleness has a purpose. Your singleness is NOT a punishment by God to make you suffer for some past transgression. Your singleness does not have to be painful or something you feel "stuck" in. For us to see progress, our singleness should have an intention. We should make our singleness operate in a particular fashion that benefits us in every aspect of our lives. We can do this by finding the purpose of our singleness.

No matter what season you're in, it's good to have a purpose rather than wander and hoping to achieve something. Single Christians must pray and ask what our purpose is during this particular season. I'm not saying it's bad to have aspirations, but it's good to seek God first and ask what He would have you to do in this season. The Bible emphasizes the importance of seeking Him first in all you do; "A man's steps are established by Yahweh. He delights in his way. Though he stumble, he shall not fall for Yahweh holds him up with his hand." (Psalms 37:23-24, World English Bible). That tells me that if we stay in God's presence, we will be kept (even if we make a mistake), and we'll achieve direction. What are some ways we can "delight" in the Lord and get guidance? Well, there are two ways:

1. Staying in the Word. Whether it's one verse a day, doing a Bible Plan in YouVersion (if you have it), or studying a specific Biblical subject you have always had an interest in will help you stay in the Word. While reading, be sure to ask for discernment and understanding and equip yourself with commentaries such as *Mathew Henry, John Gill,* or other resources that you research and prove to be credible. Don't be afraid to talk to your pastor or others the Spirit may direct you to aid in your exploration of the Word.
2. Pray with Intention. I'm aware we all have busy lives, but it's good to set aside some time to meditate on what direction your singleness is taking. The time you set aside could be as long or as short as you want it. If you want to carve out twenty-five minutes in the evening and pray for five minutes then meditate for twenty, do it! Make sure the area you decide to pray in is a space that's clear of distractions and comfortable (don't be afraid to set the mood with a candle or two or some background music if you like). When you pray and meditate, focus on what direction your singleness is taking and open yourself up to what the Spirit will say to you.

My first year of being single was a mess; I was aimless and flying by the seat of my pants. I was in church, and I did what any good church girl would do on Sundays, but the rest of the week was all about me. It wasn't until I was single for nearly two years that I felt like I was off-track. I knew I needed to do something different, but I didn't know what. After lamenting my frustration, it was kindly suggested that I pray about the matter. I thought it was silly to ask God something so trivial, but I did it anyway. I chose to pray before going to sleep since that's the time I calm my mind. Before praying, I slowed down my breathing and mentally concentrated on the purpose of my prayer. Mentally, I'd say, "what do You want me to do while I'm single" and kept saying it until I was satisfied enough to actually start praying. I didn't pray anything fancy; I just told Him how I was feeling. I continued to do this off-and-on for weeks until the Spirit spoke so clearly I thought He was yelling at me. This experience was the start of me praying with intention and was the foundation of how to develop my prayer life (more on that later). After hearing from God, I wanted to learn more about Him, which led to dive deeper into the Bible.

Reading and studying various topics in the Bible helped me get to know God's different aspects intimately. When I reviewed the commandments, I learned about His principles and what was important to Him. When I studied faith, I realized how much He esteems our trust in Him and that we choose to trust Him, especially when it's hard to do so. I also learned that He cherishes when we act on our faith because it makes us living proof of what God is capable of, and it gives Him glory. Getting to know God filled the space, and forging a connection with Him helped me be content with my singleness.

While we're in this season of singleness, we must develop ourselves spiritually. I'm not saying we have to quit everything cold turkey and be a saint. I am saying that we should let God prune us of old things and aim for progression. The next few sections will provide ways to progress spiritually and deepen your relationship with God.

Developing Your Prayer Life

I've always defined prayer as deliberate communication between God and us and, I believe it's one of the most important components of faith. Prayer encourages us (Philippians 4:6), helps us unload our burdens (Psalms 55:22), helps keep us on our guard (Matthew 26:41), and connects us to God (Jeremiah 33:3). Still, we are also called to pray as a sign of obedience (1 Thessalonians 5:17). When we pray, we speak to God directly, and He (should be) talking to us. While in prayer, our intentions must be correct, and we're not only praying so that we can try to move God for Him to give us what we want. The Word states, "You lust, and don't have. You murder and covet, and can't obtain. You fight and make war. You don't have, because you don't ask. **You ask, and don't receive, because you ask with wrong motives, so that you may spend it on your pleasures**" (James 4:2-3, emphasis added). When we pray, we must pray unselfishly. I realize how nutty that sounds, considering I just said to pray about what route your singleness should take. The difference is you're praying for the execution of HIS will and pushing what you want aside. You're saying, "Father, steer my singleness in the direction YOU want it to go. I have an idea of what I want to do in my singleness, but I want Your will to be done. Show me what you want me to do, tell me how you want me to do it, and move me to seek YOU first above all else in this season." If you were praying selfishly, there would be no mention of His will, and your intention would be for your will to be done instead of His. As you develop your prayer life, you learn to mind your motive. I researched the notion of being aware of your intentions for my first sermon and found three things to watch out for and three ways to self-correct.

Three things to look out for:

1. You pray for things out of self-satisfaction. Though desiring temporal things such as an increase in finances, a relationship, a home, or comfort aren't wrong, it becomes problematic when you're praying for these things solely for self-gratification. There's nothing wrong with you making your desires known to the Lord, but the issue lies in the fact that you only focused on what you want and what makes you feel good.
2. You place your value in the wrong things. Whether we want to admit it or not, our motives are colored by what we value. People incorrectly assume that God places as high of a value on temporal things as we do; therefore, we believe He'll give it to us.
3. You only pray when you need/want something. This one takes a little bit more self-reflection and noticing patterns within yourself. Consider the last time that you prayed to God just because. Reflect on what your last prayer focused on. It's okay to talk to God about your situation, it's okay to request God for help, and it's okay to just lay everything out on the altar, but be careful not to only go to God when there is an issue and then forget about Him until you need something else.

Three ways to stay correct:

1. Be sure to go to God with humility and to seek Him continually. 2 Chronicles 7:14 says, "if my people, who are called by my name, will humble themselves, pray, seek my face, and turn from their wicked ways, then I will hear from heaven, will forgive their sin, and will heal their land." If there's anything we know about God is that He loves a humble, repentant heart, and He loves it when you look for Him. By "look for Him," I mean immersing yourself in His word through study, meditating

on what you learn, and applying what you've learned to your life. The more you remove "self" out of the way and get to know Him, the better you'll be able to self-correct your intentions.

2. Be sure to go to Him with sincerity. Being sincere means to be free from putting on an act, being deceitful, and from being hypocritical. Matthew 6:5 says, "When you pray, you shall not be as the hypocrites, for they love to stand and pray in the synagogues and in the corners of the streets, that they may be seen by men. Most certainly, I tell you, they have received their reward." There's no point in putting on airs, trying to put on an act, or coming to God with an ulterior motive. Whether praying in public or private, don't try to be fancy or "show off." Just be transparent and be yourself with Him. Even though He knows what you're praying for or struggling with, He still wants to hear it from you. Tell Him.
3. Be sure to set your desires aside and make room for God's desire. 1 John 5:14-15 states, "This is the boldness which we have toward him, that if we ask anything according to his will, he listens to us. And if we know that he listens to us, whatever we ask, we know that we have the petitions which we have asked of him." I like this verse because it explicitly tells you that when you ask God for things, you have to make sure that they are in His will. If you are unsure of His will, consult Him through His word through fasting (which we'll discuss in the next section) and open yourself up to listen to Him when you meditate.

Ways To Pray:

Each person has their unique way of praying, and in developing your prayer life, you will find your "flow." Now, there may be a person that you admire who can pray intensely for minutes at a time without missing a beat or someone who prays softly, but something moves in you when they speak. You may find their flow appealing but be careful of that admiration turning into envy. No good will come of envy. The seed of envy will breed insecurities that can cultivate hatred, manifesting itself physically by sowing discord among other Christians. That sounds problematic, so let's not do that. The best way we check our envy is by acknowledging and accepting that the "flow" someone else has is not the same flow you'll have, and that's okay! Yes, they can pray for five hours, and the atmosphere shifts, but you may be able to pray for two minutes, and someone receives the seed of healing! That sounds good. Personally, I think it sounds great. Don't panic; there are numerous ways to help you find your "flow" and the way you like to pray, and it's so simple you're going to look at this section cross-eyed. Try these exercises, my spiritual sister, Nathifa taught me and others at a prayer workshop:

- Get yourself a package of your favorite candy that has lots of colors in it. Now assign an aspect of your life to a color of that candy. For instance, if you have a piece of candy that's red, you pray for your salvation, a yellow piece means you pray that God fills you with light, a green piece of candy then you pray for your ability to speak blessings into every aspect of your life, and so on.
- If candy doesn't work for you, get yourself a bunch of colorful ribbons and do the same thing you would do with the candy. The ribbons don't have to represent something in your personal life, but they can mean things in the world. For instance, if you have a black piece of ribbon that can represent grieving families, a brown piece of ribbon can represent people in the community, a burgundy piece of ribbon can represent the church, a purple ribbon can represent singles, and so on.
- If you like colors, try Sybil MacBeth's practice of Praying in Color. You grab a piece of paper and whatever coloring utensils that you want, and as you doodle, let your mind wander. Whatever name or situation comes to your mind as you doodle is what you pray on. The prayer doesn't have to be intricate, but it has to be genuine.
- This exercise has many moving parts and technically consists of different types of prayers, let's call it the Flow of Worship Model. This model closely follows how the Israelites would come into the temple to worship the Most High; I strongly encourage that you study this because it's interesting. When you come to your quiet place to pray, come in with a prayer of praise (thanking Him for all He's done), followed by the prayer of confession (confessing your sins and being transparent with God),

followed by the prayer of forgiveness (forgiving others who trespassed against us and forgiving ourselves), which leads into the prayer of worship (where we admonish God for who He is) and finally we come to the prayer of intercession and supplication (where you pray on behalf of others).

For the record, these are just suggestions. I encourage you to try some of these exercises and look up some things on your own and see what fits you. I didn't really figure out my flow of praying on my own until I turned 26. I like to turn the lights out, light a candle or two, sit on the floor, and sing. I don't plan the songs ahead of time; I sing whatever song that falls on my heart, and sometimes that leads into four more songs that get me into that worship mode. Once I move into worship, I do the Flow of Worship Model. Eventually, I became so accustomed to this it feels like second nature! Once you find what works, you're going to be amazed where God will take you, and you'll see what you've sown spiritually manifesting itself physically. My singleness gave me room to explore how to effectively pray in the Spirit and to examine my motives (and myself) with a magnifying glass. During my singleness, prayer kept me grounded because the more I prayed, the more God showed me what he had for me. He showed me my ministry, family, what gifts He placed in me, and what He literally shaped me to be. The hope that I received from prayer sustains me in my singleness. Keep in mind that though God will show you things, don't get too caught up in what you see. Don't get too focused on the future that you ignore the joys of the present.

The last thing we need to keep in mind is that consistency is key. This is where calendars work like a charm! Consider scheduling five minutes every day and gradually extending your time or start out dedicating twenty minutes a week then transition to a few times a week. If you want to do spontaneous prayer and don't mind how long you stay in prayer and meditation, go for it! Figure out what works for you and your schedule! If you aren't too keen on praying on your own, join (or start) a prayer group or go to a prayer service.

Fasting

Fasting is usually defined as abstaining from food for a period of time though people abstain from other things. For most Christians, fasting is a form of sacrifice and obedience, and **God delights in sacrifice**. One of my favorite scriptures that relates to this says, "For you don't delight in sacrifice, or else I would give it. You have no pleasure in burnt offering. The sacrifices of God are a broken spirit. O God, you will not despise a broken and contrite heart" (Psalms 51:16-17). The scripture says that the Lord wants more than ritualistic sacrifices, whether it's lambs, doves, goats, calves, or money; He desires an individual who's humble and willing and whose heart is set on pleasing Him. Now that's not to say that the Most High doesn't want you to sacrifice at all; He will call you to offer something out of obedience eventually. Both obedience and (real) sacrifice please Him but try to take it slow.

I understand if you're excited and charged up about showing God how serious you are about Him and how much He means to you. He's excited about your zeal, and He appreciates your tenacity, but please ask Him how He wants you to proceed with your fast. Pray and meditate about how God wants you to fast and for how long. If the Spirit moves on you to do a Daniel fast for forty days, not to eat from sunup to sundown, or skip lunch to pray for two days, do it! When fasting, it's best not to do this haphazardly. A way to help you fast with caution is by studying. Find scriptures, books, and plans that focus on fasting, its function, and what not to do on your fast. No, I am not referring to what you put in your body but how you carry yourself during your fast. The Lord rebuked Israel because though they fasted, their intention was wrong, and they did not act accordingly (see Isaiah 58:1-14). Christ even spoke about people tearing up their faces while fasting to get attention for what they're doing (Matthew 6:16-18).

Can I be honest with you? I had a real problem with being content and subtle about fasting. No, for real. I used to make posts on my social media to let people know that I was fasting. I also had an attitude during the fast because I was hungry and irked that I couldn't have my flavor blasted goldfish and ramen noodles. To make matters worse, I was commanded to step away from social media for forty days that particular year! I thought not eating was hard, but now I couldn't check my Instagram. I tried to encourage myself, but I was still petulant. When people asked me what was wrong, guess what I told them? I said, "I'm fasting" in the most pitiful, whiny voice you could imagine. Do you think God was happy with how I carried myself during my fast? Based on the scriptures I shared with you, I can firmly tell you that He was displeased. After the fact, I asked myself why did I do that? Did I act like that for attention? Did I secretly want somebody to see how "holy" I was being and how much I was "suffering"? The answer, sadly, was yes. It felt nice to get that attention, being comforted, and receiving praise for doing what's commanded of me. However, my actions did not represent the Father well, and that diminished my testimony.

If you are going to fast, do this with gladness, and please use wisdom beforehand. Don't just jump into it! Meditate and pray on it before you do it, so you don't make the same mistakes. You will probably make your own mistakes, and though setbacks don't feel good, we can learn from them, so we know not to do it again. Believe me when I say fasting gets better. It's going to be rough the first time around, and it will continue to be challenging as you progress, but it won't be unbearable. When I started fasting, I was physically and spiritually strained; but I felt the difference when I stayed consistent. When I prayed, my prayers were more profound, and I noticed that I could boldly confront my spiritual stumbling blocks. Fasting during my singleness helped me exercise self-control, which kept me from falling into sexual temptation and helped me realize that I can control my sexual desires; they don't own me. Fasting helped me purge the worldly part of me so the Spirit can fill me, bringing me closer to the Father and a step closer to contentment. While fasting, I realized I wasn't alone; not only was God with me, but I had people around me to help. Having a support system that consisted of like-minded people who're striving to cultivate their faith strengthened our bond as a group and encouraged me to stay on my A-game! My spiritual sisters and I make a group project of fasting to make the process easier (though the person who suggests starting the fast often gets the side-eye for a couple of days). Fasting is a journey all to itself that will push you in ways you never considered and will refine in ways you only dreamed of. Keep striving and brace yourself; it's going to be interesting!

Exploring Your Spiritual Gifts

Exploring is one of the more exciting things on a journey, so believe me when exploring your spiritual gifts will be a blast! You may be one of the blessed ones who knows that they're a prophetic dreamer, an apostle, or a teacher, but did you consider if you have more than one gift? Then again, you may be the individual that has no idea where to start. For those of you on the latter end of the spectrum, let's start with the basics.

Let's establish the difference between a gift and a talent. The Merriam-Webster dictionary defines talent as something naturally bestowed to you, such as athleticism, creativity, or a knack for languages. The way my sister Chante explained it to me was, "You can be a talented athlete, but you can't be a talented prophet." However, there are times when talents can be an extension of or a manifestation of your gift. Singing, for example, is known to be a talent (1 Chronicles 9:33, 1 Chronicles 25:6-7), but it can also be an extension of the gift of Exhortation (Colossians 3:16). Another example of this is storytelling. Storytelling itself is a talent, but it can also be a manifestation of or extension of your gift of Teaching (study the parables of Christ, and you'll see what I mean).

Though there isn't a set definition for spiritual gifts, let's define them as a God-given ability that the Holy Spirit grants to be used for ministry and the building of His kingdom on Earth. When the scriptures were translated from Greek to English, the Greek word used for "spiritual gift" was **χάρισμα** (*charisma*), which meant "gift of grace" or "free gift" (Strong's Exhaustive Concordance, 2020). The scriptures that contained the Greek word charisma concerning spiritual gifts were Romans 12:6, 1 Corinthians 12: 4,9, 28-31, and 1 Peter 4:10. Each of these scriptures (and more) tend to overlap in regards to specific spiritual gifts. Romans 12:6-8 lists seven gifts which are: Prophecy, Serving, Teaching, Exhorting, Giving, Leading (Administering), and being Compassionate. 1 Corinthians 12:7-10 notes nine gifts: the Word of Wisdom, the Word of Knowledge, Faith, Healing, the Working of Miracles, Prophecy, Discerning of Spirits, Speaking in Tongues, and the Interpretation of Tongues. Ephesians 4:11-13 lists the "gifts" Christ gave to guide the Church, including being an Apostle, a Prophet, an Evangelist, a Pastor, and a Teacher. These gifts are often put into three different categories though not everyone separates them, and some scholars may divide them further. For the sake of everyone's sanity, I'm sticking with the three categories (you'll notice some of these gifts overlap into other categories):

Manifestation	Motivational	Ministry
• The Word of Wisdom • The Word of Knowledge • Prophecy • Faith • Healing • Miracles • Discernment • Speaking of Tongues • Interpretation of Tongues	• Giver • Server • Being Compassionate • Prophet (i.e. Perceiver) • Administrator • Teacher • Exhorter (i.e. Encourager)	• Pastor • Apostle • Evangelist • Teacher • Prophet

In case you want context for why the categories are broken down this way,

I'm going to throw more Greek at you. When Paul talked about the gifts in 1 Corinthians 12, the Greek word **φανρωσις** (*phanerosis*) was used, and its meaning is "manifestation"; in this case, it's the manifestation of the Holy Spirit (Strong's Exhaustive Concordance, 2020). When the gifts are talked about in Romans 12, the Greek word **χαρσματα** (*charismata*) is used again. The gifts spoken of in Ephesians are self-explanatory and are offices established in the modern-day Church (depending on the denomination). I admit I'm oversimplifying the words and their meanings, but that gives you the room to study this for yourself!

Now that we've touched on the different spiritual gifts, you can start exploring what your gift is! A resource that was introduced to me by my mother was a book called *Discover Your God-Given Gifts.* Fortune's book gives you an in-depth look at how your gifts affect other parts of your life and ways for you to practice and execute your gift. Don't knock this book because it was made in the '80s; there are still some nuggets of wisdom that you can pick up! Several questionnaires help you narrow down your most dominant gift and the other gifts you have. They also breakdown the characteristics of the individual who has that gift. If you'd like to do some exploring that doesn't cost you $14.99, LifeWay Christian resources have a few free discovery tools that help you figure out your gifts and have scriptural references regarding those gifts. If those don't tickle your fancy, you can find other free assessments via search engines. Be aware, though, that each assessment is different. For instance, the number of questions may vary between 80 to 124, and the assessment itself may not list all the gifts. Some may only list seven to nine gifts, while some may list up to twenty gifts (some of which you may not have even considered a gift). When you answer the survey, it is best to respond as honestly as possible. Please don't answer it to make yourself fit into a ministry that you think you belong in. Take your time to answer these questions and know that there is no wrong answer. You may surprise yourself as to what gifts you have. I took the gift assessment made in the '80s and found out that my three dominant gifts are exhortation, intercession, and service. I was slightly surprised by my results; for instance, I thought the gift of knowledge would be at the top of my list, but it turned out to be number five! You never know what you have inside you, but now you're going to explore it!

While exploring gifts, be sure to research other individuals in the Bible who have spiritual gifts similar to yours. You may not have the same experience as that particular individual, but reading their story may help you navigate and make sense of your gift. For instance, if you're an individual who has visions, you should check out Enoch, Daniel, and Ezekiel. If you are an individual that has prophetic dreams (and/or can interpret dreams), check out Ablimech, Joseph, and Jeremiah. If you are an individual who has the gift of faith, check out Abraham, Phoebe, Lydia, Hannah, and Paul. Of course, I can mention more individuals and gifts, but I'm sure you get the idea! And of course, pray and ask the Father how He wants you to operate your gifts. Considering He's the one who gave them to you in the first place, it makes sense to ask Him how He wants you to use it and by what means does he want you to exercise and increase your gift. I want to remind you that your gifts are meant to be shared for the benefit of others. Withholding your gift may cost you bearing fruits of the Spirit, and it may cost someone receiving what they need to be spiritually healthy or to have a breakthrough. I need you to understand that the gift you have comes with the responsibility of using it to serve others to the best of your ability and the glory of God.

I found exploring and using my spiritual gifts fulfilling in my singleness. God gave me hints of my future through the gift of sight (prophecy), and I got comfort in knowing my heart's desire will be met. By developing the gift of intercession, the Spirit told me exactly what to pray for and how to pray for others in their time of need effectively. Shaping the gift of service taught me to look beyond myself to actively tend to others' needs while developing the exhortation gift helped me encourage myself more and be better in my field. Building upon the gift of discernment helped me stay out of situations that weren't good for me and increased my wisdom. The exploration and development of your gifts help you in the present and equips you for your future, whether that means ministry, elevating and expanding professionally, having a family, or other infinite possibilities! Sometimes the way God prepares us for things doesn't make sense to us, and the answer we receive (if He chooses to answer) is a riddle. I recently learned that God gives us puzzles because it makes us seek Him with more fervor, and the journey to finding the answer gives us previews of what's to come. Why the Father decides to take us through the valley, over the mountain, and across the river to get the answer is beyond me; however, I know Him enough to see that it's all for our good. You'll probably learn about one gift in the valley; conquering the mountain helped stir up two gifts, and the river refined the first gift you discovered, which will aid you in the future. In any case, you've got this! Don't worry, stay prayerful, and happy exploring!

Learning Obedience

Of all of the aspects of spiritual development, this was one of my most challenging battles. In my opinion, obedience means to comply with an order or to subject your will to someone else's; and what's the one thing a strong-willed person who has issues with authority is going to have trouble with? Letting someone else tell them what to do. The very thought of having to set aside my desires and reduce the need to do things my way was a challenge for me. I've been able to adjust better at being obedient, but I sometimes find myself trying to barter out of doing what God told me to do. For example, the Spirit told me to pray for someone who deeply hurt me. I flat-out refused and bucked against the instruction for at least four days. My mood was awful throughout those four days; nothing seemed to go right, food wasn't enjoyable, and then I felt a tugging sensation in my chest every time I thought about how I was disobedient. Finally, after my spiritual temper tantrum, I went to the altar I set up in my room and prayed for the person. After praying, I felt released from my funk and from the sting of being hurt. Take it from me, save yourself the headache, and do what He asked the first time. I've also learned that obedience has dual parts. The first part is following God's commandments, while the second is being obedient to God's will. The two components can easily intersect and merge, but they don't always do so (depending on the person). For instance, someone who's following the commandments may not necessarily be walking in God's perfect will for their life. Someone who's walking in His perfect will may not be orthodox and go against tradition (but not to the point they're rebellious or contradictory to the Word). In any case, the Lord deeply appreciates an individual who is willing to not only follow the law but also to follow in His perfect will. John 14:15 stresses that if we love the Lord, we'll obey (or keep) his Commandments, and Proverbs 3:5-6 states that we should "Trust in Yahweh with all your heart, and don't lean on your own understanding." Not to mention, the Lord doesn't think much of rebellion or rebellious people (see 1 Samuel 12:14-15, 1 Samuel 15:22-23 and Isaiah 63:10).

I realize how overwhelming it may feel to keep all of the commandments; there are 613 in the Old Testament alone and scores of instructions within the New Testament -most of which reinforces the statutes of the Old Testament. Though I have moments where I slip up, I know I'm much better than I used to be. I was a liar, stole from people, coveted what others had, was sexually immoral, selfish, the list goes on. I admit that I saw specific statutes as unnecessary restrictions, and I rebelled against them, believing I'd be free. I now realize those instructions are vital to me being a better person and being spiritually healthy. Interestingly, my journey's obedience portion didn't start with the 613 commandments but with something else entirely. During my second year of being single, I was given a specific set of instructions on how to turn my life around: the first was to refrain from alcohol, the second was to fast until He told me to stop, and the last instruction was for me to be celibate. Being obedient to just those three stipulations opened the door to things that helped shape me for the better. By not drinking, I became more resilient and practiced using more adaptive coping skills; through fasting and prayer, I got to know the Father better and being celibate helped me gain self-control and deal with deep-rooted issues. As I said, I'm not there yet, but I'm progressing, and that's what's important.

There's another piece to this obedience puzzle, and it's not one of my favorite parts. You guessed it - being obedient to those who have authority over you. That could qualify as parents, teachers or professors, bosses, pastors, government, the whole nine. Now I'm going to give you a disclaimer. I'm not a fan of how certain institutions treat those that are part of already vulnerable communities, and I will shout to the heavens about how wrong it is until the day I die. Despite that, I will expound on dealing with authority in the community and a personal level. Generally, I tend to buck against authority figures, especially if I feel as though they are wrong or if I feel I've been slighted. My behavior is even worse if I already didn't like the person! I'll yell, nearly cuss them out, and then treat the person callously afterward. I had an incident as recent as last year, where I let my emotions take over and lashed out at a person of authority because I felt as though the individual shouldn't have questioned my character. Even if I was in the right, it's safe to say that I didn't carry myself as I should have according to 1 Peter 2:13, and God wasn't pleased. I learned the hard way that there's a way to stand your ground and still honor those in authority. These are some things that helped me, and I hope they're useful to you, too:

1. <u>Take a moment to calm down.</u> Use coping skills such as taking a deep breath, using an internal countdown, or have something sensory-related in your hands to distract yourself (if possible). If worse comes to worst, don't be afraid to walk away for you to gather your thoughts. I realize that there are situations that are challenging to walk away from, such as a heated office meeting. I still suggest that you stay calm and keep your wits about you. You aren't a pushover by not losing your crap or not responding - you're wise.
2. <u>Use assertive communication.</u> Being assertive means being self-confident without being aggressive. So, using assertive communication means being confident in yourself, firm in your stance, and setting clear boundaries without being disrespectful. For instance, if someone is accusing you of something you didn't do, you don't have to shout or be deliberately hurtful to get your point across. Instead, you can state that what you're being accused of is not like your character, and you don't want to indulge in the matter anymore (especially if there isn't any proof). If the person continues to pick at you, I'd say you are free to walk away. In a professional setting, this process is tricky because your livelihood is at stake. Consider internally praying that the Spirit

helps you either say the right thing or (if you're anything like me) to hold your tongue. When the conversation segues into how you feel about the matter, take a breath and respectfully say how you feel.

There's another point about obedience that's extremely important. I need you to understand me: In the event of someone who has authority over you, whether it's a pastor, your boss, the head of your family, or your teacher is asking you to do something that is against the word of God, and your standard - DON'T DO IT! Just because someone holds authority over you does not mean they get to put you in an uncomfortable position or force you to compromise yourself. Be firm that you aren't going to do whatever they're asking you and if it escalates to the point that you do not feel safe or you're in danger, remove yourself from the situation immediately! Be sure to find someone you trust to help you and go to the police to get it documented in the worst-case scenario. I'm aware that going against the head of your family (or your spouse) may lead you to be excommunicated, and professionally it can lead to harassment or termination. It's not my intent to stir up trouble, but I intend to make sure that you are safe physically, emotionally, and spiritually.*

I get it, it's not easy to obey spiritual laws or to submit to human authority. This part of the journey will push your self-discipline limits in more ways than you can imagine as far as my boundaries have been moved, and I've still got a long way to go. I'm living proof that learning to be obedient is possible, but you won't "get" this overnight. I've been on this journey for nearly five years, and though I've done well keeping the three instructions I was given, I still find myself asking God if He's sure He wants me to do the thing He's asking me to do. Additionally, though I'm not as rude as I used to be when I disagree with human authority, the words I want to say show up on my face. No matter how far we are on our journey, we're all works in progress. Thankfully, my singleness gives me room to improve and apply the knowledge I learned. In my singleness, I learned obedience is vital to pleasing the Father, and it helps keep me on the path He has for me, even if it's hard to stay on track. Because of my desire to please Him, I'd rather stay in His will than stray and cause a ripple effect of spiritual damage. In this season, obedience taught me to exercise my faith in Him and His promises. I take solace in knowing that God is using obedience to train me to have a "Yes" in my spirit so He can use me fully in ministry later on. Keep in mind that everything you've gone through up to this point has shaped you for what's next.

Now, you may be the kind of person that the moment God says to do something, you jump up and do it. You may also be the person that if any human authority figure says to do something, you do so without grumbling, and that's great (I probably need to be in your company)! For those that still struggle, don't fret. By the power of the Holy Spirit, we're going to be victorious in this area of our lives!

*If you're in a situation where you're dealing with a hostile agent of authority: stay as calm as possible, speak only when spoken to (or say nothing), keep your voice even, keep your body language neutral, and try not to move erratically. I know this doesn't assure an individual from bodily harm, and it seems ridiculous to have to abide by these rules but do what you have to so you can see another day—your safety and life matter.

Celibacy

This aspect of my journey is the most enlightening and the most emotional for me. After being sexually active for so long, the idea of stopping seemed impossible. Sex was my power, and I was afraid of being stripped of it. To put things in context, my first experience with sex was rape, and what that did to me mentally and spiritually is another book. As I got older, I thought sex was the only way for me to get my power back, so I engaged in whatever sexual activity made me feel empowered again. I didn't realize it, but I needed to heal from what happened to me and acknowledge how that instance colored the way I saw sex. Celibacy and therapy gave me the chance to navigate through my complicated relationship with sex and helped me figure out how it impacted me spiritually. Before I move on, I want to tell you that I'm not here to tell you how you should execute your sexual agency. I am not here to shame you, and I wouldn't dare to. However, I will tell you that if you aim to please God and follow His commandments, you will have to consider celibacy. This is a touchy subject, and I can understand why; the education most Christians received about anything relating to sex was often wrought with fear, guilt, and shame. Though celibacy was taught as a way to stay sexually pure, it was presented with force, and people felt pressured to cave in to it, which contributed to the often complicated relationship between faith, sex, and intimacy. Granted, not all Christians grew up to have an unhealthy notion of sex and may have had parents or clergyman who healthily presented the concept. My goal is to present sex and celibacy to you in a way that's understanding, accessible, and attainable. It may feel like you're getting "the talk" again, but I can (almost) promise you that it won't be awkward.

Before we get into celibacy, let's talk about sex in general. Sex is amazing, and the Most High intended it to be that way. Sex is a great way to connect with your partner; it's pleasurable, beneficial physically and mentally, and helps us be fruitful and multiply! Though sex is great, there is a downside, and that downside is lust. Don't get me wrong, sexual desire and attraction are a natural part of the human experience that ranges on a spectrum from low to high. Sexual desire is defined as the state you are interested in and want to engage in sexual activity (Spector, Carey, Steinberg 1996, 175-176). The Merriam-Webster dictionary defines attraction as a draw by appeal to natural or excited interest, emotion, or aesthetic sense. In other words, attraction refers to what (or who) you find desirable. God is okay with the fact that you like 'em tall, dark and handsome or short, light and curvy! Though your preferences may have developed from your environment, He gave you that desire or interest so that you'll have a fulfilling sexual experience (or so you'll at least find the person you're with aesthetically appealing). However, that unchecked desire can lead to lust. Lust is commonly defined as an intense sexual desire, but the Bible describes lust in two ways: the lust of the flesh and the other being the lust of the eyes.

Lust of the flesh refers to craving things that physically pleasure us. Though there's nothing wrong with enjoying things that appeal to us sensually, excessively indulging in such things to the point we act sinfully is the issue. Examples of this include drugs, sex, gluttony, being drunk, and so on. Lust of the eyes refers more to the craving of people or objects that belong to someone else. Biblical examples include David desiring Bathsheba, Ahab desiring Naboth's vineyard, and Nimrod's desire for power and to conquer others. Galatians 5:19-21 describes the acts of following the flesh, "Now the deeds of the flesh are obvious, which are: adultery, sexual immorality, uncleanness, lustfulness, idolatry, sorcery, hatred, strife, jealousies, outbursts of anger, rivalries, divisions, heresies, envy, murders, drunkenness, orgies, and things like these; of which I forewarn you, even as I also forewarned you, that those who practice such things will not inherit God's Kingdom."

How does lust affect us? Mentally, it can alter how you view relationships and people. Sex is a great way to sustain a bond with a partner, but when the lust of the flesh comes to the forefront, people become gratification objects. In a neurobiological sense, being in an environment that has an (over)abundance of pleasure-seeking can lead an individual to harmful pursuits or addictions (Berridge and Robinson 2003, 507-513). In other words, the pleasure center of your brain becomes accustomed to being frequently stimulated and needs to expand measures of stimulation to be satisfied. Spiritually, it opens the door to accept anything and everything into your spirit, leading to you making detrimental decisions (David's lust of Bathsheba is a good example of this). What's more, is that you won't be able to inherit the kingdom of God (see 1 Corinthians 6:9-10). Thankfully, we've been given the tools to conquer lust, and they include the power of Christ and walking by way of the Spirit, which is following Christ's example (see Galatians 5:16). This is where celibacy comes in.

Celibacy is a voluntary vow of sexual abstinence and/or to remain unmarried though we'll be focusing on abstaining from sex. Interestingly, celibacy and abstinence aren't explicitly mentioned in the Old Testament, and premarital sex isn't stated to be among forbidden sexual acts mentioned in Leviticus 18. One theory is that the individuals in the Old Testament were expected to be virgins when married. Deuteronomy 22:13- 21 speaks about laws referring to the accusation of pre-marital sex on the bride's part and the "evidence" of her virginity (i.e., the sheet the bride bleeds on when the marriage is consummated). In the New Testament, celibacy is mentioned as a way to be holy and set apart, and singleness is described as a gift (Matthew 19:11 and 1 Corinthians 7:7-8). I believe this occurred because of the Hebrews' frequent intermingling of practices and ideologies from other cultures led to sex being seen in a more casual light, but that's just a theory. I'd be amiss if I didn't note that both Christ and Paul mention that the choice of being celibate as a life-long choice won't be for everybody due to temptation (1 Corinthians 7:2-6, 9). However, don't take that scripture out of context and run and marry whomever so that you don't fall into sexual sin. Marrying haphazardly without the Lord's guidance is spiritually, physically, emotionally, and mentally detrimental to you. There's a chance you'll hinder your ministry and growth as a person, plus you'll feel trapped. Now that the background of celibacy has been established, it's time to get into how it helps you in your singleness.

The first thing is sanctification. Sanctification is the act of making something holy. When you accepted salvation, you were also sanctified by the Holy Spirit; however, it isn't a "one and done" process. Sanctification is a life-long undertaking, and it calls for you not to do everything the world does, particularly when God finds it unacceptable. 1 Corinthians 6:18-20 says, "Flee sexual immorality! 'Every sin that a man does is outside the body,' but he who commits sexual immorality sins against his own body. Or don't you know that your body is a temple of the Holy Spirit who is in you, whom you have from God? You are not your own, for you were bought with a price. Therefore glorify God in your body and in your spirit, which are God's." As the Holy Spirit dwells in us, we must glorify God in all our ways, and celibacy helps keep our temple acceptable while we're single. The Word also says, "If anyone therefore purges himself from these, he will be a vessel for honor, sanctified, and suitable for the master's use, prepared for every good work" (2 Timothy 2:21). This verse emphasizes the importance of freeing yourself from acts and activities that will impede you from living a holy, set apart life. When we do so, we show our regard for His statutes and live in a way that shows we love Him. Sanctification is more than what I've written, so I encourage you to study sanctification and its corresponding scriptures for yourself. As a starting point, check out Proverbs 6:16-19 and check out Galatians 5:19-21 for the things the Lord isn't favorable of then read Romans 6 and 2 Peter 1:3-15.

The second is self-control. 1 Corinthians 9:25-27 states, "Every athlete exercises self-control in all things. They do it to receive a perishable wreath, but we an imperishable. So I do not run aimlessly; I do not box as one beating the air. But I discipline my body and keep it under control, lest after preaching to others I myself should be disqualified." It's easy to be complacent in being enslaved to our urges (or bad habits) because that requires no effort. On the other hand, discipline is challenging because it requires you to work against your impulses and be accountable for your behavior. Being disciplined also requires you to shift from a place of familiarity to uncertainty where there are bound to be setbacks, which is scary. In regards to celibacy, exercising self-control pushes you to go beyond physical gratification, which increases your spiritual stamina and produces fruits of the Spirit (see Galatians 5:16-24). It also shows your dedication to living a life that is pleasing to the Lord (Romans 12:1-2).

Finally, there's devotion. 1 Corinthians 7:32-35 says, "But I desire to have you to be free from cares. He who is unmarried is concerned for the things of the Lord, how he may please the Lord; but he who is married is concerned about the things of the world, how he may please his wife. There is also a difference between a wife and a virgin. The unmarried woman cares about the things of the Lord, that she may be holy both in body and in spirit. But she who is married cares about the things of the world—how she may please her husband. This I say for your own profit; not that I may ensnare you, but for that which is appropriate, and that you may attend to the Lord without distraction." In case you're wondering why the focus is more so on the unmarried (a.k.a. single people) is because without being partnered, we can dedicate more time to the Lord and for spiritual development. When you're partnered, you're often fixated on pleasing and building with that individual, and your attention is divided (this applies to those that have children and even those with active social lives). When our attention is pulled in too many directions, we compartmentalize, and some things get put on the backburner. Being celibate removes one obstacle of putting the Lord on the backburner though we'll find a way to fill that space with other people and activities. We must be careful about prioritizing other things above God and deliberately carve out time for Him, His Word, and prayer to keep us in check.

Now that we know what celibacy can do for us, here are some things to help you along the way:

- Be mindful of your triggers. Triggers, in this case, are events or situations that evoke arousal. Be honest about your triggers, whether it's people, media, or situations. My trigger is watching shower scenes with my favorite actors and actresses. There was a time I'd watch them three times in slow motion (don't judge me). Knowing that's a trigger for me, I minimized the number of times I watch the shower scenes and just let the movie or show play. If there is a place that causes a little voice in your head that sings Marvin Gaye's "Sexual Healing," please stay away from there. If there's a person in your life that turns you on and wants to turn you out, limit your solo time with them (but if they're just as bold with you in groups, RUN).

- Connect with other celibates. Though celibacy is a personal journey, the journey is enriching with a community. Although you may have sexually active friends who can empathize with you, it really makes a difference to have somebody who knows almost exactly what you're going through. When searching for a community, use your discernment to weed out the people who will feed you toxicity and do nothing but whine. I'm grateful to have spiritual sisters like Chloe, Taneesha, and Brooke to lean on when I felt overwhelmed. They prayed me up, encouraged me, and gave me Bible plans to help me stay the course. It's important to surround yourself with spiritual, fun people who have a word of encouragement for you (and be sure that you have words of encouragement for them). As Proverbs 27:17 says, "Iron sharpens iron; so a man sharpens his friend's countenance."
- Be active. Your life doesn't stop because you're celibate! Take up different hobbies, travel (if possible), or volunteer in your community. Going on prayer retreats, doing some painting, engaging in archery, and going on hikes has been a great way for me to meet new people and cultivate relationships I already had! Not to mention, it gave me a chance to explore my capabilities! This is a great time to discover what activities you find fulfilling and give you a chance to try something new.
- Pray. You're probably tired of me saying this, but this is important. In all things, pray. When this journey gets hard, and you feel like you're at the end of your rope, that is the best time to pray. I've had many moments when I was frustrated with being celibate because I believed it kept me

from living a fuller life. In those moments, I emoted and dissected my feelings to get to the root of my issue then I prayed for strength. When you feel overwhelmed, don't be afraid to reach out to your support system, whether that's your family, friends, or church family.

The journey you'll have with celibacy may be different from mine. If and when you choose to be celibate, be sure that it's YOUR choice. Don't cave in because I wrote about it or because someone else is demanding that you do it. When the Spirit and the Word convicts you, then do it. This matter is between you and the Lord; no one else fits into this equation. I'm living proof that it's possible to celibate and still enjoy your life. If I, the former chieftain of whoredom and foolishness, can be celibate and satisfied, so can you. Remember, we can do all things through Christ who strengthens us!

II

Personal Development

Introduction

Do you know what's one of the most amazing things about life? It's the fact that things are rarely stagnant. Celestial bodies are often in constant motion, weather patterns shift, and plants undergo various changes, as do animals. Humans fall in line with going through constant changes, but humanity can choose to change or not! We can choose to move forward or backward or to be static. How does this relate to your singleness? Personal development is a major portion of maturing as an individual; without it, you'll become "stuck." It's easy to go through life, turning a blind eye to our flaws and deficits, and bury the responsibility of exposing and dealing with them. I'm not saying that you have to claw through every aspect of your life to find faults, but I'm saying that if there's something you know you need to heal from, improve upon, or get to the root of, now is the time to do it.

Don't let the fear of the unknown paralyze you into not moving forward. Confronting and trying to move past traumas and disharmonies in your life can be scary and uncomfortable, primarily if you worked hard to repress it, but taking steps to heal yourself is empowering. If you want something different to happen in your life, consider improving negative issues and your mindset. This undertaking will be challenging, but you'll see its value once you notice how much lighter you feel and no longer feel bound. Let's break these chains one link at a time.

Learn About Yourself

Are you familiar with those quizzes that'll let you know what kind of latte you are, what breed of puppy you'd be, or what Disney villain represents your soul? I think some people (including me) like those quizzes because we're hoping to get better glimpses of ourselves, or we're looking to affirm what we think we know about ourselves. Getting to know yourself is beneficial for your well-being. The ability to reflect on what motivates you, what you value, who you are, and why you behave a certain way is the key to confidence and improving yourself. Though being self-aware requires a level of work, this process doesn't have to be grueling! As you continue through this section, there'll be exercises to help you get in touch with yourself.

Everyone has something they value, whether it's material or immaterial. Values are things that determine how we live and function. Whether you want to acknowledge it or not, your values drive you to make certain decisions, live a certain way and affect the way you see the world. Many of us have values that stemmed from our caregivers or our environment, and some of our values were bred from experiences we had. Being able to explore the root of your values will help you understand yourself as a person. During one of my supervisions at work, my director had my colleagues and I do a Core Values exercise. We were presented with a list of values and given three to five minutes to pick out words that stuck out to us, then prioritize our top three values out of the list. The words that stuck out to me were:

fairness, justice, kindness, faith, community, arts, personal growth, love, nature, purpose, beauty, fun, joy, friendship, and health. Out of this list, my top three values are personal growth, fairness, and joy. After much thought, I realized personal growth is important because it provides room for improvement and contentment. Fairness is important to me because I believe it helps people see beyond themselves and extend kindness to others. Finally, joy is important to me because it helps me appreciate the little things in life, which keeps me anchored during hardship. This exercise allowed me to unearth and analyze my values, and I'd like to extend that to you. There are numerous lists of values you can pull up from any search engine ranging from 50-200 values. Whatever list you choose, please read it thoroughly, write down all of the words that stick out to you, prioritize your top ten, and then explore why you find those things so valuable. Although the task seems simple, I found it quite challenging, especially with only prioritizing three values. As you do this exercise, you may surprise yourself with what you consider valuable. Exploring your values is an integral part of getting to know yourself, but it doesn't compare with getting in touch with your emotions.

Identifying your emotional states and recognizing how your body feels while in those states will increase your self-awareness. One way to guide you through this process is a prompt. The prompt should be simple, can be applied to various emotional conditions, and best done in a calm state so you can contemplate with clarity. An example of a prompt would be something like this:

- What makes you angry?
- What's your body language like when you're angry?
- How does your body feel when you're angry?
- What's your behavior like when you're angry?
- What helps you to calm down?

Doing this kind of prompt helps increase your emotional awareness by identifying triggers (things and events that set off emotions) and noticing the physiological changes in your body while experiencing various emotional states. I've followed a similar prompt my job provides us, and it helped me identify my triggers, make a calming plan for myself, and empowered me to manage my emotions effectively.

Another way to get to know yourself is to identify your various communication styles, such as your argument style. Whether you're an individual who avoids conflict or not, we all have an argument style. Figuring out how you approach and handle conflict will help you develop better (i.e., non-destructive) arguments with others. Our argument style is often shaped by our environment, our experiences, and even our personality. For instance, if you grew up in a household where your caregivers avoided conflict at all costs, that may have rubbed off on you, and now you're avoidant or shut down when stressful situations occur. However, if you ever tried to stand up for yourself in your childhood and you were brutally shut down, that may have led you to avoid conflict or directed you to be more determined to stand up for yourself. In the event, you grew up in a household where everyone yells and screams at each other, your argument style may be more aggressive (which can also meld into your personality). There are different argument styles that I didn't mention, and there are free resources available for you to explore what your style is. If you're similar to me, you may find yourself going down a rabbit hole of filling out various tests such as the Relationship Attachment Style Test, Humor Styles Questionnaire, and the Big Five Inventory. When filling out any questionnaire, it is best to answer the questions truthfully. We all love to see ourselves in a positive light, but if we want to get to the truth about who we are, we will have to be honest, even if that means the less desirable aspects of ourselves are revealed.

While you're exploring aspects of your personality, you might as well explore what your love language is! Gary Chapman's book *The Five Love Languages* has been all the rage for decades, and it's understandable why that is. The book is a good resource to help people get an in-depth look at how they desire to be loved and express love to others. Thankfully, Chapman's website allows you to take a love language quiz for free, and they have an assessment, especially for singles! I take the quiz annually to see if my results change, but it's been consistent for three years. My primary love language is quality time, followed by acts of service, physical touch, words of affirmation, and receiving gifts. The benefit of knowing my love language is gaining confidence in making meaningful connections and increasing my ability to communicate my emotional needs better. Knowing how important it is for others to be attuned to my needs encourages me to learn about others' needs, so they feel loved and appreciated.

In addition to finding your love language, figuring out your passions will help you get to know yourself. Engaging in other interests will help enrich your life, provide you with an outlet to channel your stress, and give you the chance to exercise skills you normally wouldn't use. For you to figure out your interests, you have to ask yourself some more questions. What activities excite you? What activities do you love doing? What activities do you find relaxing? Is there a social cause that you feel drawn to? Do you care about medical research or treatment of specific diseases or disorders? What places would you consider volunteering your time to? Would you go to animal shelters or wildlife reserves? How about peer-support or mentoring groups? Does supporting food banks, blood banks, hospitals, or places of worship appeal to you? There are many other avenues for you to explore your interest but don't get stuck on the idea that there's only one thing that you can be interested in. Be flexible and open to the idea of treading unfamiliar territory; you may be pleasantly surprised at what you'll find satisfying. I've found joy in trying things like paintball and volunteering at church and citywide events. I've even tapped back into my love of performing and discovered I enjoy modeling (and I'm pretty good at it)!

Discovering yourself and your interests is a lifelong process, and it's something that shouldn't be rushed. As you become self-aware, your self-confidence will gradually increase because you're more sure of who you are and what you want. That sense of empowerment will never be taken away from you once you get it. Even when the narrative of being single isn't enough is pressed on you, you'll now have the strength to push back and live unapologetically. Don't underestimate the treasure of knowing yourself. After all, Proverbs 3:13-14 states, "Happy is the man who finds wisdom, the man who gets understanding. For her good profit is better than getting silver, and her return is better than fine gold."

Dealing With Toxic Traits

Let's define toxic traits as behaviors that negatively impact your quality of life. A quick list of harmful traits includes being hostile, being unforgiving, being prideful, projecting onto others, being self-disparaging, being resentful, lying to yourself and others, throwing temper tantrums when angered, making yourself a martyr, not respecting others boundaries or your own, being manipulative, being envious, condemning others, backbiting, baiting others to anger, using people for self-gratification, and not being accountable. I'm sure there are more traits I've missed, but you get the idea. Every single one of the traits is just a prevalent symptom of the real issue. If you have deep-rooted problems that you refuse to face in your singleness, they will surface in your relationship(s). Though it may take years to bubble up, all it takes is one trigger for it to explode. When it explodes, you're now tasked with dealing with that trait, maintaining your relationship(s), and sustaining your quality of life simultaneously. You cannot ignore those toxic traits and expect them to disappear in any relationship. If you know the behavior is negative, and you don't like it, you can't expect someone else to put up with it and be satisfied. These traits aren't just something you can squash down in hopes they'll never surface. I tried doing this for years, and all it brought me was anxiety and disharmony. Some of us are living in this reality and keep falling into these adverse cycles because of it. So, how can we free ourselves from these tendencies and break the cycle?

1. Identify the Issue. This seems like a given, but people may not have the time to delve deeper into why they are the way they are. While you're able to focus more on yourself in your singleness, carve out the time to look within and note negative patterns that occur in your life. Start with keeping a journal of negative behavioral trends you notice about yourself. When you've written your findings, take one issue and then start exploring when the pattern emerged and how that issue manifested. Note if that pattern occurs close to a traumatic event, a significant change in your life, or if it developed from your environment or upbringing. It'll be challenging for single parents or caregivers to set that time aside to explore those depths. The only thing I can suggest is turning to your support system to help unburden you for a period of time or schedule blocks of time you want to dedicate to this step.
2. Research. When you have your epiphany and figure out the issue, find books and materials geared towards that particular issue. Seeking the aid of a professional can help you navigate through this process. If a professional is out of the question, there are some mental health resources and support groups available to help you (I'll put some resources in the back of the book).
3. Make a Plan. This process is not passive. It makes no sense for you to have all of this wealth of information about yourself and then do nothing with it. If you want to heal, you have to establish what you're willing to do and how much work you're ready to put in to be in a better headspace.

I'm not encouraging you to do anything that I haven't done myself. I made a list of maladaptive behaviors I had, and the most prevalent one was my anger. It didn't take much for me to be angry as a child. Still, there was a certain point where my anger branched off into other behaviors such as being mistrustful, emotionally fragile, engaging in risky behaviors, being emotionally abusive, and hostile. With some reflection, I realized the root of my anger was bitterness from being sexually assaulted and harboring ill feelings towards the individual who assaulted me. I made up my mind that

I wanted to heal and believed forgiveness was the first step. Since the task of forgiving this person seemed impossible, I wrote out a chart to help me understand the pros and cons of forgiveness and steps to achieve my goal:

Reasons I don't want to forgive	Reasons why I should forgive
• I don't want to put in the work for something that wasn't my fault • I feel like I'm being passive about what happened • I'm being too soft • I feel like I deserve to be angry • It feels like I'm giving the person who assaulted me a "pass" • I'm scared that nothing will change even if I do forgive him • I've defined myself by this hurt and I don't know how to live without it	• I don't like the "guck" inside me (bitterness, anger, sadness) • I'll be released from perversion • I'll feel freer and I'll have peace • If I can forgive him then it'll be easier to let go of grudges • I deserve to not feel suffocated by the past

<u>Steps for Forgiveness</u>

1. Feel the feelings and let them out:

- Reflect (on the situation).
- Reveal (the feelings you felt then and now).
- Release (in a safe space with someone you trust or alone).

1. Acknowledge the feelings of the incident and the aftermath:

- Use "I" statements ("I felt…" and "I thought…").

1. Write the reasons why I should forgive and why I don't want to:

- Further dissect each reason, if possible.

1. Ask uncomfortable questions:

- Do I really want to forgive?
- Am I ready to forgive? Why or why not?

1. Study forgiveness and what it means to forgive:

- Read scriptures.
- Read psychology journals.
- Read other survivor's stories.

1. Every day make an active decision to forgive (and explore what that looks like).
2. Pray and fast for this issue.

I shared what I wrote down to give you an example of making a plan and dissecting your reasons for wanting to heal and why you don't want to. If you'd instead make a flowchart, list, or a mind map, do that! If you want to use my table and steps as a template, you can do that, too! All that matters is finding the best way to organize your thoughts and make a visual of your steps to heal. The further I went into my healing journey and getting more in-depth in my faith, I realized it was time to step out of the "this is who I am" rhetoric. That issue is **not** who I am, but I've identified with it for so long it became part of me, and I couldn't tell the difference between me and it. That thing meshed with my spirit for so long it hurt to let it go, and I was scared to live without it because now I'm vulnerable. I thought my anger was a fortress; snapping at others kept the "weak" people away, and building walls was protecting me, but instead, I built a prison. It took years of fasting, prayer, and professional help to break down the barriers and allowing the Lord to fill the space left behind. Make a choice to ask God to expose those issues and where the cracks and crevices are and let Him fill them. Please don't place the unrealistic expectation that your would-be partner, friends, or loved ones will heal and fill those deficits. God is the only one that can do that; please let Him.

Wellness

Wellness is defined as the quality or state of being in good health, especially as an actively sought out goal (Merriam-Webster, 2020). Generally, when most people hear "wellness," they may picture physical health, but it's so much more than that! Wellness has many aspects, and each one affects your quality of life. As wellness dimensions are explored, we'll discover why each aspect is important and how to enhance it.

Generally, physical wellness refers to our bodies' proper care to have optimal body and brain functioning. Why is this important? Being physically healthy means lower health risks, better weight management, maintaining muscle strength, aid in mental health, and more. To achieve these benefits, we must adhere to three things, exercise, proper nutrition, and rest. I'm aware that we live in a world that's full of processed foods (which are more affordable), long work hours that don't leave us much time to do anything else, and we're chronically exhausted, yet the quality of sleep eludes us. Considering all that, what can someone do to increase physical wellness? First, go to a physician and get yourself a check-up. Suppose you don't have insurance, research urgent care centers, walk-in clinics, or community clinics that are inclusive and fit your financial needs. Next, make a similar table that you made for dealing with toxic traits. List your habits, note why you need to change, and the possible setbacks you'll face. Following that, research tips that promote good sleep hygiene, healthy nutritional habits, and exercises that fit your health goals. Finally, make a plan. You don't have to make a grandiose plan; start with baby steps. For example, I made a plan to prep and cook my meals for the week on Sundays. For physical activity, I carved out twenty minutes to go for a brisk walk or do an exercise routine I found on Youtube. For sleep hygiene, I made a bedtime routine to prepare my body for sleep, which consists of me getting a cup of lavender tea, turning out the lights, meditating for five minutes, and then putting on rain sounds in the background.

According to the World Health Organization, mental wellness refers to the level of someone's psychological and emotional well-being. It encompasses coping skills, learning capabilities, processing situations, and relating to the world (and others). Why is this important? The core of mental wellness is having positive coping skills and being resilient. If you are an anxious individual and panics, it could lead you to make rash decisions or direct you to avoid the problem leaving it unresolved. Regarding coping skills, maladaptive (negative) coping skills such as self-medicating, self-harm, eating disorders, and the like will give you the feeling of being in control, but the impact of those strategies will add to or exacerbate the problem. Not to mention, your general well-being will be affected in the long-term. Not being able to relate to or perceive others will build a barrier to connect with other people truly. To foster romantic, familial, platonic, and professional relationships, we must understand different perspectives, learn to be vulnerable (with the right people), extend kindness and truly listen to others. To improve mental wellness, engage in self-reflection, pray and meditate, revamp your coping strategies, seek professional and spiritual help, talk out your feelings, and make a plan with steps to help conquer the issue.

Let's define emotional wellness as the ability to self-regulate, be self-aware, and be self-accepting. Why is this important? It's not healthy to go through life either repressing your emotions or letting your emotions control you. Flying off the handle or shutting down when things get tough will not benefit you in relationships or in general. Finding a balance between acknowledging and expressing your emotions in a controlled manner takes time and work. A proactive approach calls for identifying your feelings then using coping skills before reaching your breaking point. Taking the time to know my body cues when I'm reaching an emotional state helped me initiate my coping skills proactively. Some coping skills I use are counting, taking a walk, listening to music, or going to a different area and relax. Another approach is making a back-up communication plan to convey your emotions when words are hard to use. Keep some writing utensils nearby, but consider making code words for various emotional states if that's challenging. For example, if your emotions are at a heightened state (but it's not anger), your code word could be "yellow light." If your emotions are at an intensely heightened state, your code word could be "red light." Whatever code words you choose, make sure your loved ones and friends are aware of those words' meanings so they can help and act accordingly. Share with them what you're doing and why you think this will help. When you're able to calm down and communicate, make sure you use "I" statements. Rather than saying, "You made me upset when you..." instead try saying, "I felt upset when..." I've found using "I" statements empowering because it helps me take responsibility for my feelings. When you speak, make sure your voice is calm and your tone is even. The other person may not be as receptive if they feel like you're blaming them (even if it is their fault). Suppose the other person gets defensive and makes you upset, use your coping skills, and walk away if you have to. Though I would suggest, you warn the other person that you're going to walk away before things get out of hand.

The University of Maryland defines intellectual wellness as engaging in mentally-stimulating and creative pursuits. Keeping your mind active helps with maintaining cognitive functioning, and you become a more well-rounded person. Other benefits include shaping your own thoughts and opinions (not following the crowd), getting in touch with your creative side, challenging your ideas, boosting your critical thinking skills, helping you with rational decision-making, understanding other perspectives, and so much more. Simple ways to increase your intellectual wellness (some of which are my favorite things to do) include reading books, doing puzzles, starting a project, finding a new hobby, debating with some friends, learning a language, and taking a random course! If reading books isn't your thing, audiobooks will come to the rescue. If jigsaw puzzles aren't your thing, there are brain games you can download, crossword puzzles, word games, card games, or board games you can play. Improving intellectual wellness will probably be the most fun thing you'll do in this area unless you don't like learning. If you're that person, I'll be praying for you.

Spiritual wellness refers to the morals, ethics, and beliefs a person may hold that steer their life and give them purpose (University of Maryland n.d.). Considering the first half of the book discusses ways to develop spiritually, I won't go into too much detail. However, here are some suggestions on improving our spiritual wellness: dedicating time to help the community, giving to those in need, taking the time to pray and meditate, fast, connecting to nature, showing gratitude, not condemning others, and being obedient to the commandments.

Other forms of wellness I felt were worth mentioning are professional enrichment, creating an aesthetic (or beauty) regimen, and decluttering. Developing yourself professionally will expand your skillset, maintain your proficiency, and build your confidence. Exploring if your values align with your occupation, taking courses relevant to your field of work, reexamining your career plan (or revamping your career altogether), and taking steps to further your career such as going back to school can help you progress professionally. Creating an aesthetics regimen for yourself will help you structure your time and give you an excuse to take care of yourself. Not to mention, you'll give yourself a mental health and confidence boost! Decluttering your space could be both figurative and literal, but either way, it's constructive. Figuratively, decluttering in your life means removing things, people, and habits that aren't benefiting you. Literally, decluttering gives you a chance to restructure your space, which may relieve some tension and lead you to feel accomplished and refreshed. I didn't mention other forms of wellness, but that gives you a chance to seek them out for yourself.

Overall, wellness is a state of being, and maintaining it is a life-long process that requires a lot of effort. I'm grateful I delved into wellness during my singleness because I've been able to focus on myself, and I have room to achieve personal growth without too many distractions. Making the conscious decision to increase your quality of life and follow through with it is quite the undertaking. If you find following through with your plans challenging, be sure to have a healthy support system to encourage you and connect with like-minded others. You can do it; I believe that Christ will give you the strength to move these mountains!

Minding Your Money

Though this topic could go under wellness, I thought it deserved an entire section. When I say "mind your money," I'm referring to saving and budgeting your money for the short-term and long-term. Managing anything in your life requires you to have wisdom and be prudent, and your finances are no different. The Merriam-Webster dictionary defines wisdom as having experience, knowledge, and good judgment and being prudent as acting with care and considering the future. Proverbs 21:5 says, "The plans of the diligent surely lead to profit, and everyone who is hasty surely rushes to poverty." I'll admit that I was not diligent when it came to financial matters! I'd save money like a champ and be prudent initially, but it didn't take long for me to reach a slippery slope, and the money was gone. I learned the hard way (several times) that money management is a crucial component to feeling secure and can improve your quality of life. People in vulnerable communities may not have access to opportunities to reach financial stability, but some fundamental things can help anyone get a leg up.

The first is to set short-term and long-term financial goals. A short-term financial goal is a target that you can achieve within a couple of years or less. Such goals can include saving up for a car, establishing a vacation fund (which your bank can help you with), or raising funds to pay off various bills. A long-term financial goal is a target that will take a few years or more to reach. Such goals can include saving money to buy a house, paying for your education, starting a business, or saving for retirement. Some goals like saving money to pay off debt or saving for a down payment can either be considered a short-term or long-term goal. After setting your goals, there are several things you can do to figure out how you should proceed:

1. Prioritize. You need to take the time to sit down and set up which goals you want to work on first. If it helps you to write a list of long-term and short-term goals, please do so. After establishing your goals, you'll have an idea of how to budget, so you're able to meet your goals.
2. Check Your Credit Score. Something that can make or break your financial goals is your credit score. Your credit score can open doors for you to receive lower interest rates on loans, credit cards with better terms, and other financial benefits. You can request your credit report free every twelve months on annualcreditreport.com, or you can download a credit monitoring app to keep tabs on your credit score. If you need to boost your credit score, there are scores of blogs, websites, and services at your disposal, but be sure you do your research.
3. Learn. One of the best things I could have done for myself was to take a financial literacy course. Though I took an in-person class, there are other options available! The Federal Deposit Insurance Corporation (FDIC) website has a financial education program called Money Smart. The program is computer-based instruction for young adults and adults, has 11 modules, and the program is free! All you have to do is register on the Money Smart page, and you can start the course right away and go at your own pace. There are other programs and classes at your disposal, be sure to do your research and use the one that fits you!

Next, make lists of your expenses. In the finance course I took at Temple University's PASCEP program, the instructor told the class to chart our average monthly fixed expenses, flexible expenses, and monthly income. Some of the charts I made looked something like this (for the record, this is a composition of averages of bills and things I made up):

Fixed Expenses	Cost
Car Payment	$213
Health Insurance	$112
Rent	$1300
Internet/Cable	$55
Total	$1,680.00

Flexible Expenses	Cost
Food	$300
Gas (for the car)	$115
Cosplay Materials	$600
Materials for Jewelry Making	$28
Total	$1,043.00

Doing these charts helped me realize how expensive I was, that I didn't plan well regarding unexpected expenses, and gave me the chance to reevaluate my spending. As you reexamine your various expenses, consider adding your tithes, savings, and retirement accounts to one of the lists. Another exercise from that finance class was making a chart of our debt. The group was tasked to write who we owed, how much we owed, and the interest of what we owed (if there was any). I looked through all of my paperwork for bank loans, credit card debt, student loans, auto loans, and even IOUs to make sure my chart was accurate. The following is an example of a debt chart:

Owed To	Balance	Interest	Monthly Payment
FedLoan	$8,514	6.800%	$50.18
FedLoan	$4,829.25	3.400%	$16.13
Citizen's One	$5,654	5.700%	$190.66
Ray Ray	$250	N/A	-
Bank Credit Card	$885	11.15% (APR)	$23.00
Macy's	$54	27.49% (APR)	$28.00
Total	**$20,186.25**		

My list was much longer than this, and the total was more intimidating. Though seeing how much debt I was in initially hurt my feelings, viewing the breakdown of how much I owed encouraged me to tackle my debt. Making this chart inspired me to explore debt-reduction techniques (like the high-interest rate or snowball method) and tailor a plan that fits my current financial situation. As you formulate your plan, keep those long-term and short-term goals in mind.

Whether you want to take on another source of income or know your options, a professional financial adviser could help you answer some questions and reach your goals. If you don't know where to start finding a financial advisor, ask friends and family for recommendations, search for advisors on reputable databases, or search via general search engines. It may also help you have an accountability partner to help you stay focused on meeting your goals. If you'd like to learn or continue educating yourself about investing, there are several resources at your disposal. The (free) Money Smart course touches on investing, there's *Stock Investing for Dummies* by Paul Mladjenovic, and there are various blogs and websites such as Business Insider! If you're curious about other kinds of investments, consider talking to your bank about Certificate of Deposits, retirement plans (whether you have a workplace plan or not), or mutual funds if they have them. Investing is still new to me, and I can't give you an expository for something I'm still learning, but that's the fun of studying things for yourself! As you're exploring these concepts, you're not only gaining knowledge to improve your finances, but you're increasing your intellectual wellness!

The relationship you have with your finances doesn't have to be a rocky one. Singles need to gain as much knowledge about finances, in general, to provide themselves with more security. Since singles are more likely to be stressed due to shouldering all financial responsibility, it's important to grasp where our finances stand and how to move forward. As you read and learn, don't forget to keep Christ at the forefront. There was a point I was so fed up with the financial setbacks that I felt hopeless and became depressed. Things got so bad that I had to fast and pray for the yoke to break off me. I'm sharing this with you so you know you aren't alone feeling hopeless or frustrated. I'm also telling you this so you don't fall into the same trap I did. I forgot Philippians 4:6, which says, "In nothing be anxious, but in everything, by prayer and petition with thanksgiving, let your requests be made known to God." When I surrendered my anxiety about my finances over to God and engaged in Spirit-led tithing, everything changed. I didn't feel like I was drowning in worry anymore. I had a brighter outlook knowing that God was sustaining me. I took the educational opportunity He presented me with, which led me to make wiser financial decisions. By the grace of God, I've paid off thousands of dollars of my debt; my credit score makes me feel bourgeois, I have a retirement fund, and I saved enough money to put towards my Master's degree. If you are in a season where the bills are mounting up, and you feel like you're drowning, don't feel hopeless. I pray that God proves Himself to you as a provider and will sustain you throughout this season. I'm living proof that things won't always be this bleak. God's got you and has a plan that's meant to give you hope and a future; please hold on.

Conclusion

Have you ever heard the story of Jairus's daughter found in Mark 5 or the son of the widow of Nain found in Luke 7? Both Jairus's daughter and the widow's son in Nain were dead before Christ came but, when He arrived, He commanded them to rise, and they lived. Interestingly, besides not mentioning their names, both stories never said what happened to the young people after being raised. I imagine that neither of them could live their lives the way they used to. After being raised from the other side, something about them had to be different! Whether they felt physically different or became more attuned to spiritual things, nothing had to be the same as before. When these two young people were raised, I believe they left some things in the "dead place." You are similar to Jairus's daughter and the widow's son. You were once dead in something, but Christ called you to raise you into something better. Being raised to something better means that some mindsets and behaviors need to be left in the "dead place." Leaving behind something you were comfortable with carrying will feel strange, but it'll be odd trying to hang on to something you've outgrown.

As you spiritually and personally progress, the "old you" will shed like dead skin but, just like dead skin, there will always be remnants hanging on to you that you won't see. It's going to take a special substance to expose the remains and remove them for good. For us, that particular substance is Christ. Your singleness is the best time for Christ to expose and free you from things that have kept you in bondage. Being single allows you to be self-aware, improve yourself, and live as authentically as you allow.

The lessons I've learned in my singleness helped me create a recipe for a spiritual foundation that ended up blessing me in every aspect of my life. What recipe will you make from the ingredients of singleness?

Bibliography

"8 Dimensions Of Wellness". 2020. *Live Well @ UMD*. Accessed November. https://umwellness.wordpress.com/8-dimensions-of-wellness/.

Berridge, Kent C., and Terry E. Robinson. "Parsing reward." *Trends in neurosciences* 26, no. 9 (2003): 507-513.

Fortune, D. and Fortune, K., 2009. *Discover Your God-Given Gifts*. Grand Rapids, MI: Chosen Books.

Merriam-Webster.com Dictionary, s.v. "function," accessed August 11, 2020, https://www.merriam-webster.com/dictionary/function.

Merriam-Webster.com Dictionary, s.v. "talent," accessed September 21, 2020, https://www.merriam-webster.com/dictionary/talent.

Merriam-Webster.com Dictionary, s.v. "attraction," accessed November 5, 2020, https://www.merriam-webster.com/dictionary/attraction.

Merriam-Webster.com Dictionary, s.v. "wellness," accessed November 18, 2020, https://www.merriam-webster.com/dictionary/wellness.

Merriam-Webster.com Dictionary, s.v. "wisdom," accessed December 27, 2020, https://www.merriam-webster.com/dictionary/wisdom.

Merriam-Webster.com Dictionary, s.v. "prudent," accessed December 27, 2020, https://www.merriam-webster.com/dictionary/prudent.

Spector, Ilana P., Michael P. Carey, and Lynne Steinberg. "The Sexual Desire Inventory: Development, Factor Structure, and Evidence of Reliability." *Journal of Sex & Marital Therapy* 22, no. 3 (1996): 175–90. https://doi.org/10.1080/00926239608414655.

"Spiritual Assessment Tool: Discover Your God-Give Spiritual Gifts." LifeWay Christian Resources, September 10, 2015. https://www.lifeway.com/en/articles/women-leadership-spiritual-gifts-growth-service.

Resources

Books

Abused Boys - The Neglected Victims of Sexual Abuse by Mic Hunter (Ballatine Books, 1993).

The Gaslighting Recovery Workbook: Healing From Emotional Abuse by Amy Marlow-MaCoy LPC (Rockridge Press, 2020)

Healing Sex by Staci Haines (Clies Press, inc., 2007).

Men and Grief: A Guide for Men Surviving the Death of a Loved One: A Resource for Caregivers and Mental Health Professional by Carol Staudacher (New Harbinger Pubns Inc, 1991).

Healing The Soul Wound: Counseling With American Indians And Other Native Peoples by Eduardo Duran (Teachers College Press, 2006).

The Unapologetic Guide To Black Mental Health by Rheeda Walker (New Harbinger Publications, 2020).

Websites

Bella DePaulo

Is a Social Scientist whose current title is "Academic Affiliate, Psychological & Brain Sciences, UCSB." She's a life-long single who's dedicated her life to study singlehood and destigmatize singleness. http://www.belladepaulo.com/

HealGrief

Is a free online resource for those who are grieving and need support to navigate through their distress. They also have additional resources if virtual support doesn't fit your needs. https://healgrief.org/virtual-support/

Healthy Philly Minds

Is a free online mental health resource for Philadelphians from every walk of life.

https://healthymindsphilly.org/en/resources/

The National Alliance on Mental Illness (NAMI)

HelpLine: 267-687-4381 (dial 1)

https://namiphilly.org/nami-other-support-resources.html

Trauma Survivors Network

c/o American Trauma Society
201 Park Washington Court
Falls Church, VA 22046
Toll Free: 800-556-7890
Local: 703-538-3544
admin@traumasurvivorsnetwork.org
https://www.traumasurvivorsnetwork.org/traumapedias/organizations-resources

About the Author

Elizabeth Sowell is a servant of the Lord and the author of *Ingredients Of Singleness*. She's been single since the latter half of her twenties and has hit the ground running ever since. She's a mental health professional who's currently pursuing a Master of Science in Education - Special Education with an Applied Behavior Analysis concentration at Saint Joseph's University. Elizabeth loves nature, reading, singing, and enjoys daring adventures such as white water rafting and archery tag.

You can connect with me on:

- https://bookofe.com
- https://www.instagram.com/book.of.e

CPSIA information can be obtained
at www.ICGtesting.com
Printed in the USA
BVHW041734220221
600782BV00006B/642

9 780578 846880